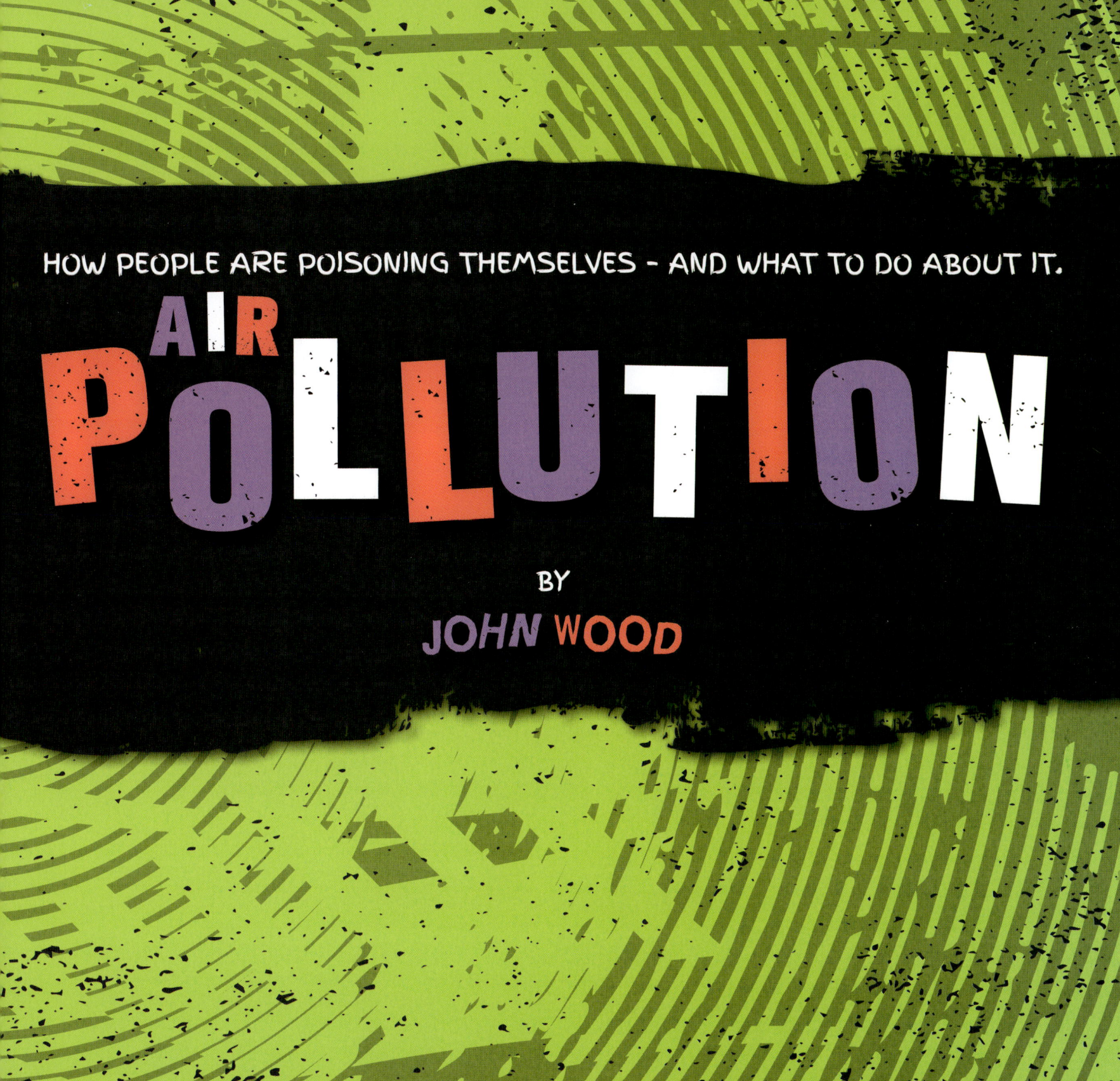

BookLife PUBLISHING

©2021
BookLife Publishing Ltd.
King's Lynn
Norfolk PE30 4LS

All rights reserved.
Printed in Malta.

A catalogue record for this book is available from the British Library.

ISBN: 978-1-83927-454-1

Written by:
John Wood

Edited by:
William Anthony

Designed by:
Danielle Rippengill

All facts, statistics, web addresses and URLs in this book were verified as valid and accurate at time of writing. No responsibility for any changes to external websites or references can be accepted by either the author or publisher.

Image Credits

All images are courtesy of Shutterstock.com, unless otherwise specified. With thanks to Getty Images, Thinkstock Photo and iStockphoto. Cover: wow.subtropica, Rayyy, sokolovski, Milan M, NickolayV, NadyGinzburg. 4 – Guntsoophack Yuktahnon. 5 – Hung Chung Chih. 6 – Tatiana Grozetskaya. 7 – photowind. 8 – NadyGinzburg. 9 – Parilov. 10 – CGN089. 11 – Gelpi. 12 – Vasily Smirnov. 13 – insta_photos. 14 – 3355m. 15 – Gr-Siamidis. 16 – Ziablik. 17 – FotoKina. 18 – andras_csontos, eggeegg. 19 – sirtravelalot, LeManna, NDAB Creativity. 20 – Riccardo Maye. 21 – Diyana Dimitrova, Mimadeo, risteski goce. 22 – Hung Chung Chih. 23 – Chinnapong.

CONTENTS

PAGE 4   Breathe

PAGE 6   What Is Air Pollution?

PAGE 8   What Causes Air Pollution?

PAGE 10 A Danger to People

PAGE 14 A Danger to the World

PAGE 18 Stop Air Pollution!

PAGE 20 Renewable Energy

PAGE 24 Glossary and Index

Words that look like this can be found in the glossary on page 24.

BREATHE

Oxygen

Carbon dioxide

Breathing is important. We need to breathe all the time to live. Our bodies breathe in **oxygen** from the air and breathe out **carbon dioxide**.

It is important that the air we breathe is clean and safe. If there are dangerous things in the air, this could be very bad for people.

What Is AIR POLLUTION?

When the air becomes mixed with harmful things, we call it air pollution. When air pollution levels get high enough, the outside air can become dangerous for people to breathe.

Big cities often have lots of air pollution.

Soot also adds to air pollution.

There are all sorts of things that can create air pollution, such as dangerous gases or pollen.

What Causes Air Pollution?

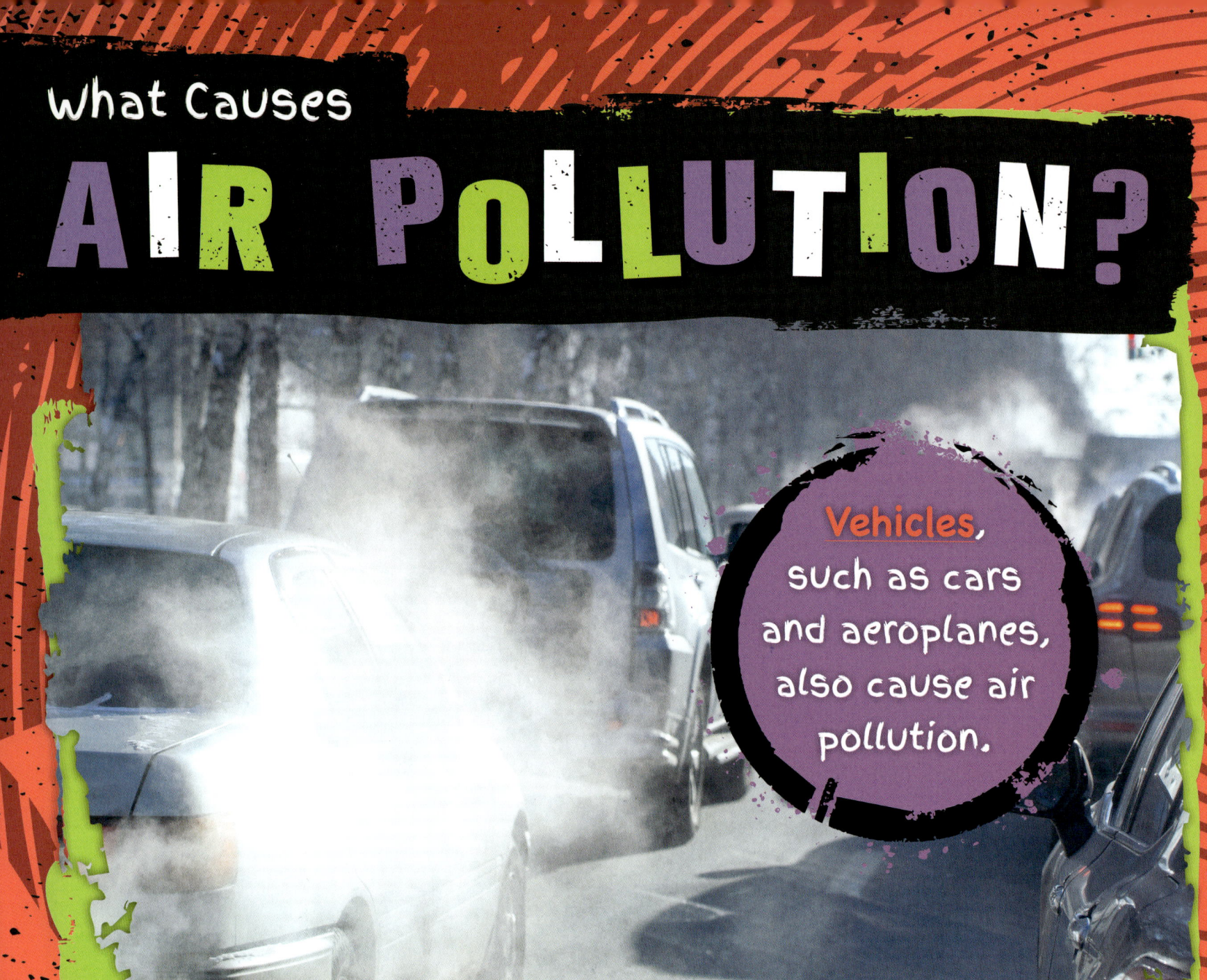

Vehicles, such as cars and aeroplanes, also cause air pollution.

Air pollution is usually caused by things that people do. For example, many factories cause air pollution.

Many countries burn **fossil fuels** for electricity. This creates a lot of harmful gases. This is just one important reason that people should stop using fossil fuels.

This is coal, which is a fossil fuel.

A DANGER to PEOPLE

Air pollution can be especially dangerous to elderly people.

Air pollution can cause some problems straight away. If someone has asthma or damaged lungs, air pollution can make it difficult for them to breathe.

There are problems for healthy people too. Healthy people might feel dizzy or sick because of air pollution. People have also said it can cause headaches.

People might get a cough, or their eyes and throat might feel sore.

Air pollution can cause problems that people only notice years and years later. After enough time, the lungs or heart can become damaged.

It is thought that air pollution can be harmful to babies when they are born.

Air pollution can cause diseases such as **bronchitis**. It might even cause a very serious disease called **cancer**. These kinds of problems might mean people live shorter lives.

A DANGER to the WORLD

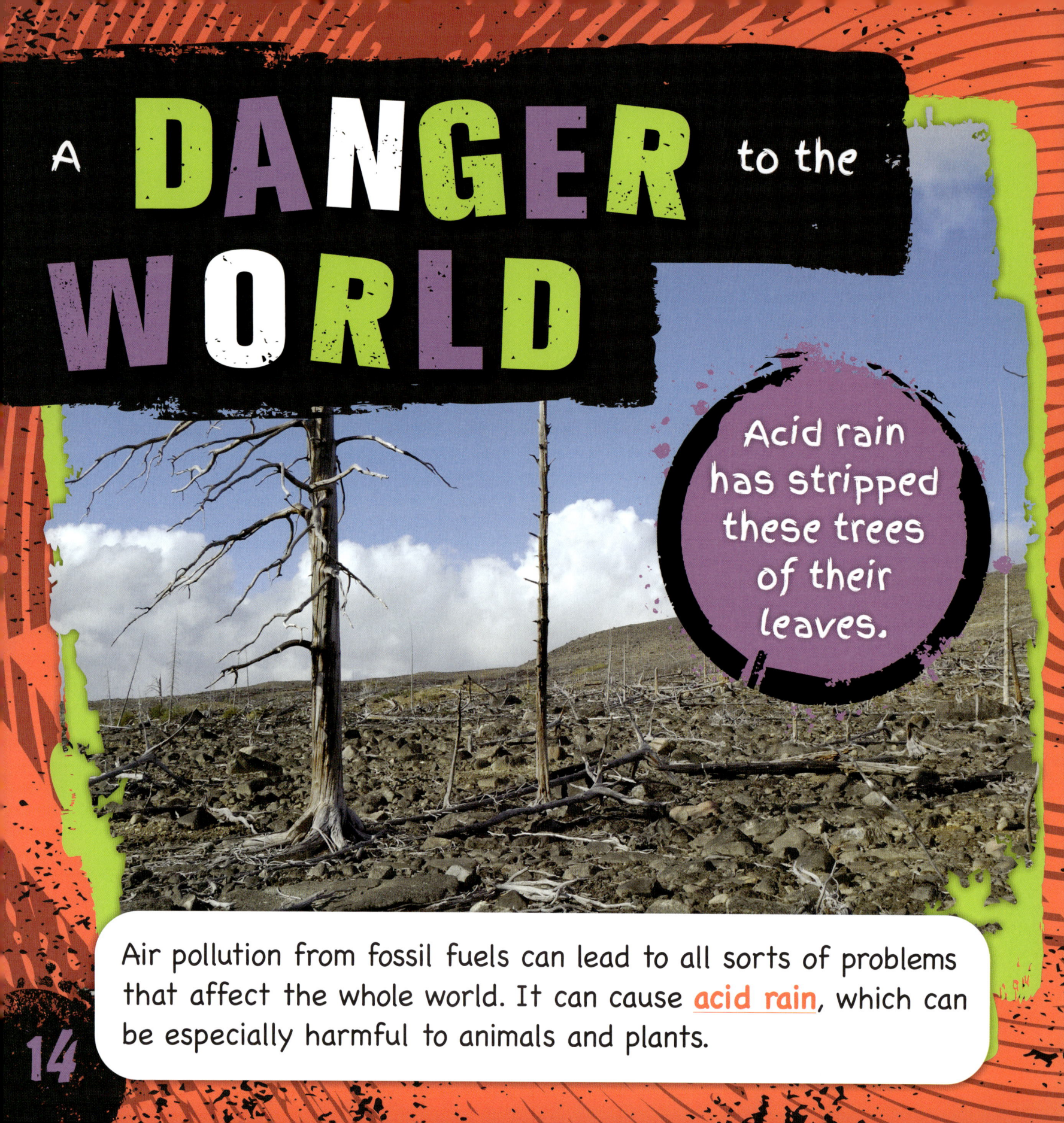

Acid rain has stripped these trees of their leaves.

Air pollution from fossil fuels can lead to all sorts of problems that affect the whole world. It can cause **acid rain**, which can be especially harmful to animals and plants.

It is not dangerous for humans to walk in acid rain. However, the **chemicals** that cause acid rain are harmful to people when they are in the air.

When acid rain falls on lakes and rivers, it can make them too dangerous for animals to live in.

Burning fossil fuels creates greenhouse gases. These gases get mixed into the air and trap lots of heat from the Sun. This warms the world up and causes something called climate change.

Climate change causes more extreme weather, such as hurricanes.

This is a hurricane in the US.

Climate change causes problems for people. One problem is that the <u>polar ice caps</u> are melting. This causes sea levels to rise, which means land near the sea may soon start to flood.

Stop AIR POLLUTION!

One way to stop air pollution is to use less electricity. This means less fossil fuels will be burnt.

Turn off lights when you aren't in a room.

Make sure TVs and computers are completely turned off – not just on standby.

Another way to stop air pollution is to travel less in cars and aeroplanes.

Walk or cycle instead of using the car.

Ask your family if you can go on holiday in your country, so that you don't need to take an aeroplane.

Get the bus or train more. The more people who share a vehicle, the better it is for the world.

RENEWABLE Energy

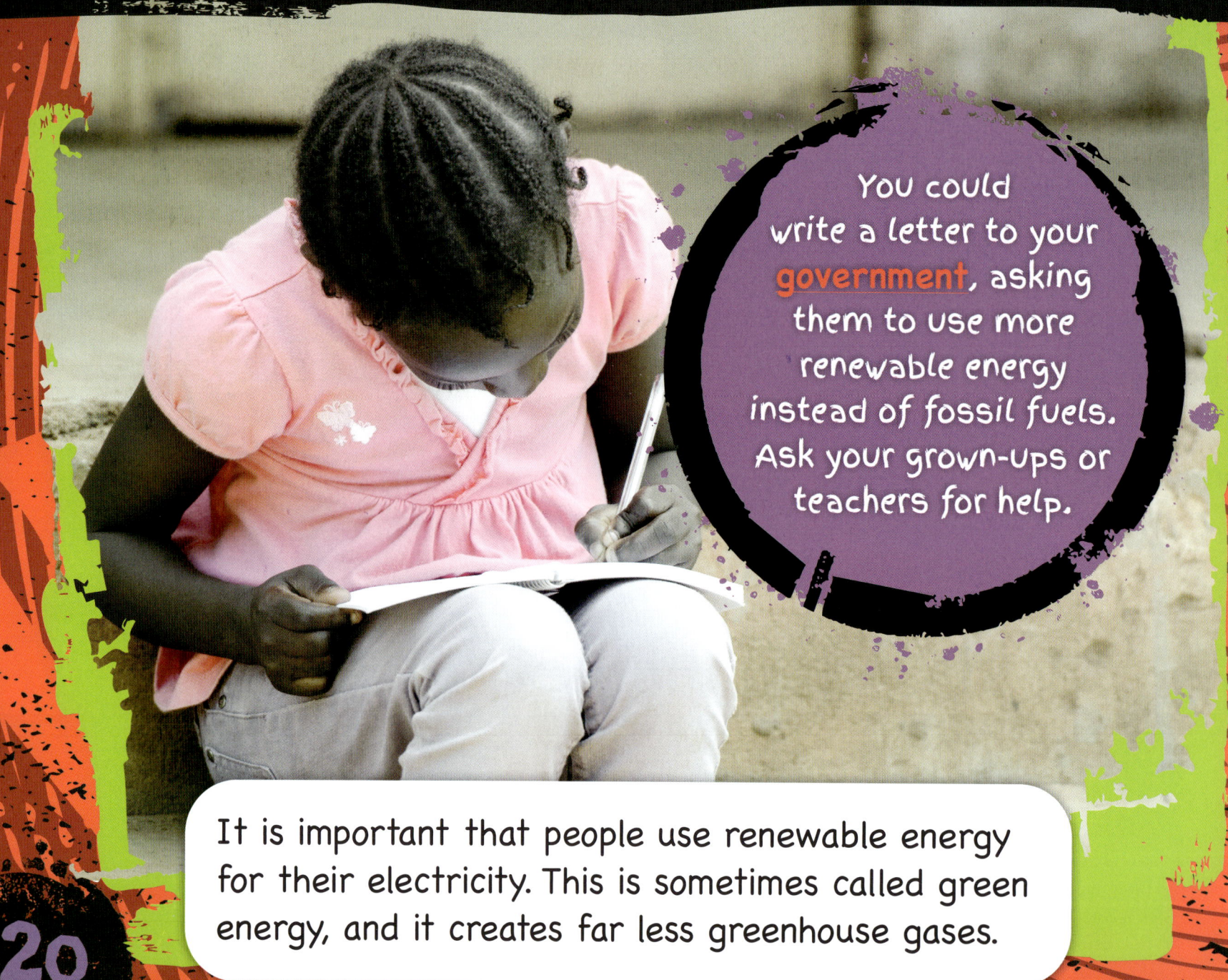

You could write a letter to your government, asking them to use more renewable energy instead of fossil fuels. Ask your grown-ups or teachers for help.

It is important that people use renewable energy for their electricity. This is sometimes called green energy, and it creates far less greenhouse gases.

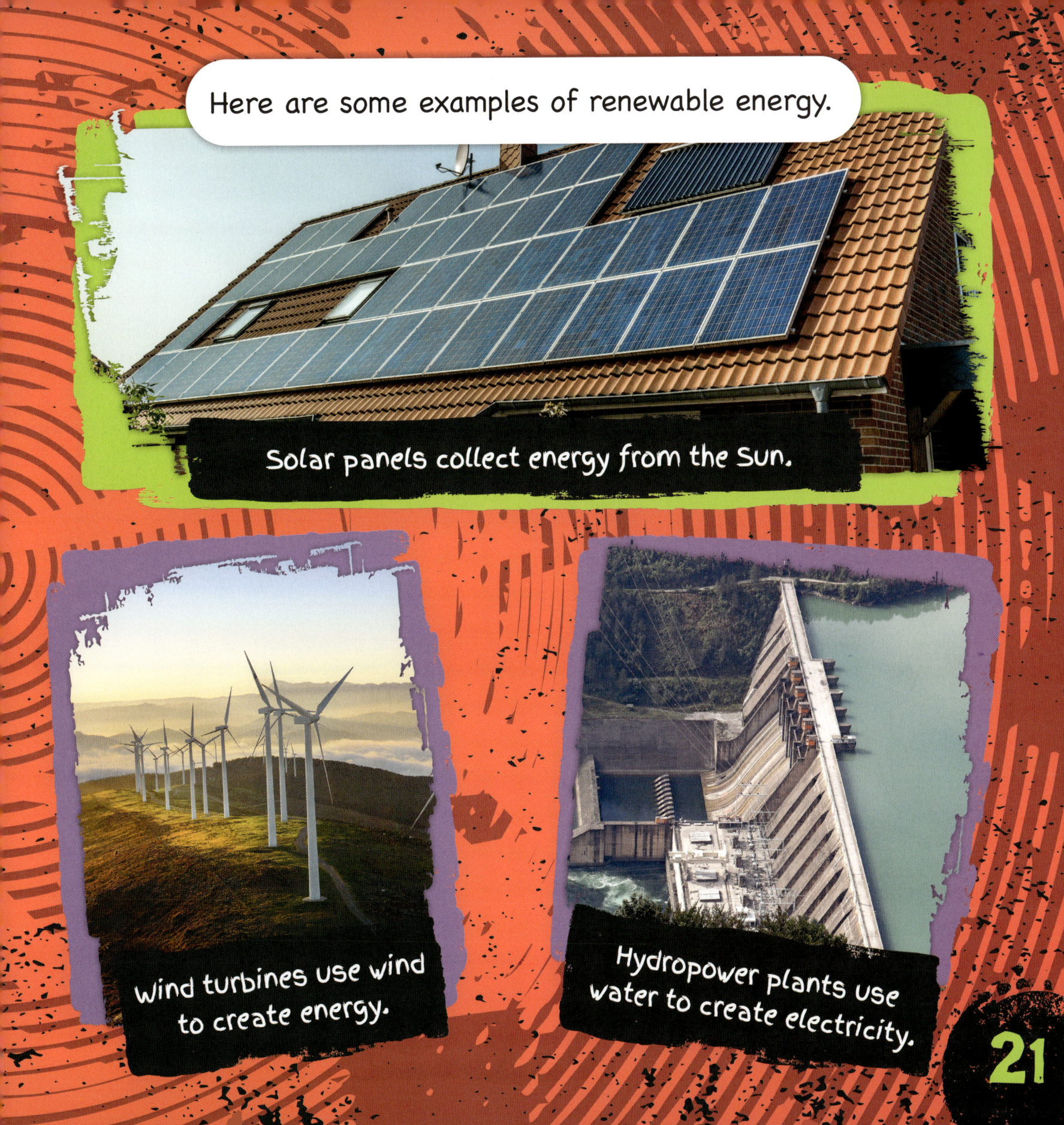

Some buildings and cars have machines to clean the air. These are called air filters or air purifiers. They can be helpful in making very polluted air a little bit safer.

Air purifier

Air filters can help people in dangerous areas. However, it is important that people look after the world and make sure there is little or no air pollution there in the first place.

GLOSSARY

acid rain — rain that is made acidic by pollution in the atmosphere
bronchitis — a disease that affects the air pipe
cancer — a serious disease which involves growths in the body
carbon dioxide — a natural gas that is found in the air that humans breathe out
chemicals — things that are usually made by scientists
fossil fuels — fuels, such as coal, oil and gas, which formed millions of years ago from dead animals and plants
gases — things that are like air, which fill any space available
government — the group of people who are in charge of a country
oxygen — a natural gas that living things need in order to survive
polar ice caps — the sheets of ice at the top and bottom of the Earth
pollen — a powder that is used by plants to make new plants
vehicles — machines that have an engine and are used to carry people or things

INDEX

air purifier 22
animals 14–15
asthma 10
climate change 16–17
coughing 11
electricity 9, 18, 20–21
factories 8
green energy 20–21
headaches 11
heart 12
lungs 10, 12
plants 14
vehicle 8, 19
weather 17